ISBN 978-1-330-34253-4
PIBN 10034006

This book is a reproduction of an important historical work. Forgotten Books uses state-of-the-art technology to digitally reconstruct the work, preserving the original format whilst repairing imperfections present in the aged copy. In rare cases, an imperfection in the original, such as a blemish or missing page, may be replicated in our edition. We do, however, repair the vast majority of imperfections successfully; any imperfections that remain are intentionally left to preserve the state of such historical works.

For support please visit www.forgottenbooks.com

1 MONTH OF
FREE
READING

at

www.ForgottenBooks.com

By purchasing this book you are eligible for one month membership to ForgottenBooks.com, giving you unlimited access to our entire collection of over 1,000,000 titles via our web site and mobile apps.

To claim your free month visit:

www.forgottenbooks.com/free34006

COMPARATIVE RELIGION

ITS METHOD AND SCOPE

A PAPER READ (IN PART) AT THE

THIRD INTERNATIONAL CONGRESS

OF THE HISTORY OF RELIGIONS
OXFORD, SEPTEMBER 17, 1908

BY

LOUIS HENRY JORDAN, B.D. 1855

AUTHOR OF
'COMPARATIVE RELIGION : ITS GENESIS AND GROWTH'
'THE STUDY OF RELIGION IN THE ITALIAN UNIVERSITIES,' ETC.

HENRY FROWDE
OXFORD UNIVERSITY PRESS
LONDON, EDINBURGH, NEW YORK, TORONTO AND MELBOURNE

1908

OXFORD: HORACE HART
PRINTER TO THE UNIVERSITY

p3099

SECTION IX
THE METHOD AND SCOPE OF THE HISTORY OF RELIGIONS

THE METHOD AND SCOPE OF COMPARATIVE RELIGION

THE title of this Paper, it will be observed, has been slightly altered since it was submitted to the Executive Committee. In its original form it read: 'The Relation of Comparative Religion to the History of Religions.' Inasmuch as the Congress had hitherto confined itself to the discussion of topics falling within the province of the History of Religions, it was necessary to choose a theme that would not seem to conflict with that well-established practice. When however it was found that a great many accessory papers were available on the present occasion, the Committee decided to inaugurate an entirely new 'Section' of the Congress. It then became possible for me to vary the heading of my paper in accordance with this altered understanding; and, although our actual subject remains unchanged, I have made a distinctly desirable substitution of titles. If the one selected prior to the formal creation of Section IX were retained, and I were now to read this Paper as a contribution originally intended for that Section, my action might seem to imply that Comparative Religion was nothing more than a branch of the History of Religions. My sole aim, however, to-day will be to show that every such theory is based upon a serious misapprehension! It seems necessary, therefore, to recast somewhat the phrasing of my subject. The contrast about to be drawn between the method and scope of two related disciplines will probably be the best means of revealing their essential and fundamental differences.

The question to which we now address ourselves is introduced for the first time at one of these International Congresses. The initiation of this discussion, and the frank recognition of its importance, are notable signs of the times. The step we are taking is in no sense premature. A difficult problem has been confronting students of religion for a considerable period, and the embarrassment of the situation has been steadily growing. If we shall find ourselves able to reach and register a verdict, or if our present discussion should succeed only in making more clear the principles that underlie a widely prevalent diversity of opinion, we shall assist in removing an issue by which many are still perplexed, and in lending impetus to a line of inquiry that desires and deserves our help. To me, it is a source of unbounded satisfaction that room has been made in our programme, this year, for several papers that deal expressly with Comparative Religion. One reader [1] has chosen for his subject ' A Science of Comparative Religion', and I know in advance that he is going to bring us an affirmative answer to that query. It has long been one of my dreams that I might yet see this vast and expanding department of investigation accorded that place and prominence to which it is entitled. The action of the Executive Committee of this Congress—their courageous new departure, reference to which has already been made—cannot fail to contribute materially towards the realization of this hope. Further subdivision of the work undertaken by these quadrennial conferences will eventually follow, with results of the very first importance for the prosecution of our studies.

I. *The Methods and Scope of the Science of Religion.*—It is desirable that, for a moment, we should make a retrospective glance. Let us recall, as a preliminary step, the methods and scope of the Science of Religion. It is essential that one or two of the considerations which such a survey suggests should be clearly borne in mind.

By 'The Science of Religion' we mean that increasing group of studies, diverse yet closely interrelated, by which man is seeking to unravel the mystery of his religious acts and aspirations. In particular, the Science of Religion is the product of the deliberate investigation of the facts of religion—and of *all* the facts, whatever their relative age, number, or consequence—when these data are dealt with in accordance with some clearly defined scientific *method*.

These methods have varied very greatly, and naturally they have been applied with varying degrees of proficiency.

1. The Historic Method.—The special type of inquiry which is at present most widely in use—the oldest if reckoned from the date of its introduction, and more fruitful than any other if measured by the

---

[1] Mr. I. Abrahams, of Cambridge.

harvest it has won—is known as the historic method. This mode of investigation takes scrupulous account of the *objective* facts of religion. Facts of religious ritual, the substance of oral or written beliefs, facts connected with sacred places, facts associated with sacred persons—these and a great host of kindred items of information fall to be accumulated, and then competently examined. Moreover, every such fact—be it trivial or important, crude or profoundly suggestive, a mere memory that is recalled to-day by some persistent survival, or a significant contemporary act that evokes invariable reverence—*every* such fact is collected, duly recorded, and supported by such proofs as furnish it with its necessary credentials.

2. The Psychological Method.—Another process of dealing with the facts of religion—one of the latest to be introduced, but already very extensively employed—may be denominated the introspective or psychological method. Here the factor of man's *inner experiences,* whether such experiences be those of the investigator himself or of other beings like himself, is given the place of primary importance. In harmony with the demands of this particular method, the inquirer seeks to arrive at the determining facts of religion by laying bare their hidden psychological bases.

3. The Comparative Method.—A third mode of research, and one which students of the Science of Religion ever increasingly employ, is the critical or comparative method. In this instance—the facts of religion, alike objective and subjective, having been accumulated in a fairly satisfactory measure—the investigator proceeds to determine their *real* agreements and differences, their points of demonstrable interdependence or of equally demonstrable originality, the standards of relative excellence aimed at, the goals either missed or attained, &c., &c. It will be seen that this line of inquiry comes necessarily late in the history of the Science of Religion. It presupposes the application of certain preliminary methods. While it reserves its right to review in any given case the conclusions reached by those who furnish it with its immensely varied materials, it depends admittedly upon auxiliary helpers for its data. These data it gratefully accepts and utilizes in accordance with its own definite purposes.[1]

[1] It will be understood that, in these sketches of three important scientific methods, no attempt is made to do more than characterize each in broad and general terms. It will be understood, moreover, that various other methods, successfully employed by experts in this field, are equally deserving of mention and praise. My aim has been merely to single out, and emphasize, three *distinctive* methods. The selections I have made are purposely representative, and may be regarded as fair illustrations of all the others.

The natural result of utilizing different 'methods' in the study of the phenomena in question has been the gradual development—within the Science of Religion—of a series of distinct 'departments', bearing such names as *The History of Religions, The Psychology of Religion, Comparative Religion,* and so on.

Until recently, these various methods of research have very often been pursued simultaneously. They have been employed, in varying measures, by the same investigators. The scholar who collected the facts of religion proceeded, as he had opportunity, to compare those facts one with another, to determine (as well as he could) their material and psychological origin, to note their points of likeness and unlikeness, &c., &c. But such an immensely exacting task has not usually been achieved with any conspicuous success. On the contrary—to put the matter positively—this haphazard mode of procedure has become responsible for conclusions so subjective and unreliable that it is now very generally being abandoned.

As a consequence, the various 'departments' of the Science of Religion have tended, more and more, to drift asunder. Each has become ambitious to pursue uninterruptedly its own quest in accordance with its own particular method, and to enlist the guidance of trained workers who would be in a position to devote to it their undivided effort.

II. *The Relation of Comparative Religion to the History of Religions.*—It was inevitable that, sooner or later, the relation of the various 'departments' of the Science of Religion—their relation not only to the central corpus of this study, but their relation to one another—would have to be determined. The question we have to consider to-day is the relation of *Comparative Religion* to the *History of Religions.* Two main theories on this subject widely prevail. Let me state and examine them in their order.

1. The theory of subordination.—The older view—and, thus far, the predominant view—declares Comparative Religion to be plainly subordinate to the History of Religions. For it is alleged, and it is quite correctly alleged, that nearly all the material with which Comparative Religion busies itself is derived from the History of Religions. All its prominent representatives are obtained from the same source. In a word: it is said that Comparative Religion would never have been heard of, if it had not been for that other department of inquiry from which now it aspires to be separated.

2. The theory of equality.—The second school of opinion is constituted by those who hold that Comparative Religion stands upon a platform of perfect equality with its older and stronger colleague.[1] It maintains that the History of Religions—although it appeared first in the order of time, and although the fundamental character of its work must always ensure its outstanding prominence—has no warrant, on these grounds merely, to claim an unquestioned pre-eminence. Priority of advent and control does not suffice to create a lawful monopoly. In other words: it is declared that the scope, authority, and general executive functions of the History of Religions, hitherto interpreted in a decidedly generous way, must now be made subjects for review.

By those who accept the former of these theories, Comparative Religion is regarded as a mere *adjunct* of the History of Religions. Indeed, this habit of invariably attaching Comparative Religion to some other subject has had a good deal to do with raising the current question whether this study is not fully competent to stand by itself. It is notorious that a remarkable diversity of sentiment has been found to prevail—I hope I may say, without offence, a ludicrous diversity of sentiment—touching the way in which this troublesome adjunct might best be disposed of. Thus, in various colleges and universities, it has been taught in connexion with Church History, or Oriental Literature, or Oriental Philosophy, or the Philosophy of Religion, &c., &c. In theological colleges, it is usually dealt with to-day under the head of Apologetics,—a procedure which, while capable of vindication on certain grounds, is open to serious objection.[2] Comparative Religion is still taught after this manner in England, in Scotland, in Canada, and in numerous colleges of the United States. In the latter country, however, as we shall see in a moment, a new order of things is being rapidly introduced. Separate university 'departments' for the scientific study of religion are being created, and efficiently equipped in the matter of professors, instructors, libraries, seminars,

[1] There are many who think that Comparative Religion occupies the higher platform of the two,—a platform considerably higher, and one that is steadily rising! But these enthusiastic souls I omit from our present survey.

[2] It is a great mistake to create the impression that Comparative Religion exists, and is chiefly to be cultivated, for the purpose of strengthening one's theological defences. Such a view is entirely misleading. Comparative Religion may indeed be made very effective in the service of Apologetics, but it has no direct interest in the vindication or undermining of dogmas, whether Christian or non-Christian.

&c.[1] It is in special Schools of this type, intended primarily for the training of competent teachers, that the problems peculiar to Comparative Religion are likely ultimately to be elucidated: and in taking the forward step which has just been referred to, America has set an example which—in such varying ways as may be suited to their needs—other countries would do well to imitate.

Happily a movement of the same sort, though more limited in its range, has already begun to manifest itself in Europe. The practical difficulties which have arisen in connexion with every attempt to foster Comparative Religion in association with some other subject have led many to conclude that it ought in future to be developed as a separate academic discipline. It was quite natural and legitimate that, for a time, Comparative Religion should have been studied as a sort of by-product of the History of Religions. But this relationship—convenient, happy, and even essential, at the outset— ought not to be unduly prolonged. It would seem better that these two great domains of inquiry should now be deliberately divorced. Such action, moreover, would be not only reasonable, but timely. Comparative Religion has begun to organize, in various tentative ways, a special equipment of its own. It can point already to a small band of competent and devoted workers. It has made a beginning, likewise, in the direction of providing for its students a distinctive and accredited literature.

III. *Contemporary tendencies which increase the necessity of separating Comparative Religion from the History of Religions.*—The theory that Comparative Religion is a study entirely subordinate to the History of Religions, while everywhere accepted a quarter of a century ago, is now practically outgrown. It is becoming widely recognized that these two departments of the Science of Religion must in future be dealt with separately. In order to emphasize and promote the growing change of opinion which is rapidly taking place, the following facts—contemporary in their character, but none the less important on that account—are entitled to be taken into serious consideration.

1. The too rapid popularizing of the study of the History of Religions.—When students of religion first deliberately set to work, it often proved extremely difficult to procure the data of which they were in quest. No books on the subject could be had, and the scanty information obtainable was fragmentary and unreliable. At the outset, the conclusions which these pioneers reached were com-

[1] Cp. p. 16.

municated almost exclusively to the membership of learned societies. By and by, a few of the more ambitious leaders ventured formally to publish the results at which they had arrived. Perhaps it was better that these portly and unattractive tomes did not secure many readers: for their contents were incomplete, inexact, and often positively erroneous. But the persistent inquiry went on. More worthy treatises superseded these earlier ones, imperfect records were in course of time revised and amplified, and errors were gradually eliminated. Thus the world has come into possession of its numerous standard *Histories* of religions, in which each Faith is expounded by various competent interpreters, and in harmony with the requirements of the highest type of scholarship. It was in this way that, after more than half a century of toil, we have gained our best current expositions of Brahmanism, Buddhism, Confucianism, Mohammedanism, &c., &c.

But, within the last few years, the study of religion has entered upon an entirely new phase: for the printing press has been so used as to awaken a distinctly *popular* interest in the subject. One can purchase now in England an authoritative account of any of the religions of the world for the trifling expenditure of a shilling![1] Moreover, such books are found to meet with a prompt and steady sale. The same experiment is being made, and with similar energy, in Germany.[2] What has been the result? As the outcome of this new campaign on the part of the press—and of other organizations also, as I shall show in a moment—the leading facts concerning all the great religions have now been scattered broadcast. The daily newspapers, as well as the monthly magazines and reviews, are lending additional impetus to the movement. And, as is most natural, everybody is now busily *comparing* these facts! Persons who are wholly unburdened by the discipline and enlightenment of collecting the material in question, who possess no special qualification for sifting it, who—in some cases at least—have utterly failed to understand it, are much the most conspicuous students of Comparative Religion at this hour!

But agencies additional to the press have been busy in the work of rapidly popularizing the leading facts of religion. A pertinent

---

[1] Take, for example, *Religions Ancient and Modern.* 21 vols. London, 1905- . [*In progress.*] Or, at a very moderate cost, within the compass of a single volume, *Religious Systems of the World.* London, 1890. [4th edition, 1901.]

[2] The best illustration may be found, perhaps, in the immense circulation secured by certain volumes of the series known as *Religionsgeschichtliche Volksbücher,* now in course of publication at Tubingen.

instance may be found in the ' Hall of Religions' which—with its
effective tableaux, lectures, &c.—was one of the special features of
the recent Orient Exhibition in London.[1] It is quite true that
Professor Haddon of Cambridge, and other responsible directors,
stood sponsor for this novel and difficult undertaking; and, on
the whole, the experiment was conducted with a gratifying measure
of success. But, of this somewhat daring venture, one outcome—
unintentional no doubt, but unmistakable—has been the serious
check it has given to the advance of Comparative Religion. The
purpose of that science has been grossly misconstrued, its method
has been misapplied, and its scope has been very inaccurately
appreciated.

Or let us take, as an illustration of the same general peril, the
recent formation in London of the Buddhist Society of Great
Britain and Ireland. This association constitutes a Branch, and
is likely soon to become an important Branch, of the International
Buddhist Society. Few will challenge the right of this group of
students to pitch their tent among us, or to publish that popular
series of Tractates in which they are now expounding *The Message
of Buddhism to the West*.[2] For my part, I wish them well: whatever of light and leading they may be able to communicate to the
citizens of this Christian land, they should not only be permitted
but encouraged to impart. Again, however, it will be remarked
that, under the impulse of a foreign and unexpected influence, two
World Faiths are now being deliberately contrasted. Thus the
disposition to make comparisons of differing religious systems, without ensuring at the same time that such comparisons shall be valid
and searching, is being continuously fostered. Is it any wonder
that, yielding unconsciously to the force of so many conspiring
circumstances, the comparison of man's beliefs is now actually taking
place every day? The exponents of Comparative Religion seem
suddenly to have sprung up everywhere! Yet, less than ten years
ago, neither the name of this science, nor the practice of it, was
more than very occasionally mentioned, and then only in circles
that were exclusively academic.

In view of the deliberate effort which is now being made to
popularize the study of religion—an effort which, even already, has
reacted very disastrously upon the interests of Comparative Religion—

---

[1] Held during June and July, 1908.

[2] Begun in 1908. See *Buddhist Sermons*, which also date from the present year.
The *Buddhist Review*, the official organ of the Society, will begin publication a few
months hence.

I appeal to this Congress to come to the assistance of those who are seeking to put this new study under the supervision of competent and responsible persons. This is no paltry plea for the recognition of threatened and invaded rights, or for the bestowment of honour upon workers who have hitherto been ignored or overlooked. My appeal is based upon considerations of an entirely different character. It is not the vested interests of Comparative Religion, but the abuses which are at present endangering the progress of all branches of the Science of Religion, that I have especially in view. Students of the History of Religions may be counted upon, I am sure, to lend assistance in rescuing Comparative Religion from the ills that now seriously menace it. The abuses in question have become perilously rife of late. If, therefore, a remedy is to be found, it must be found quickly: and it can be applied effectively only by emphasizing, and emphasizing sharply, the differences which separate two great departments of advancing modern inquiry.

2. Contemporary insistence upon specialization.—It is often said that the historian of religion is the man best equipped for dealing with the problems of Comparative Religion, seeing that he has already all the necessary facts at his finger-ends. But this statement errs greatly by way of exaggeration. The historian of religion has not yet accumulated all the data which it is his bounden duty to collect; and, what is more, he has only partially assimilated the material which he already possessess.

Many who are listening to me to-day are aware that, on the other side of the High Street here in Oxford, in one of the strong rooms of Queen's College, there rests a pile of boxes containing miscellaneous papyrus documents. These writings, obtained from those ancient depositories in which the *Logia* [1] of Jesus were recently discovered, remain still unopened : for Professor Grenfell is reluctant to take the time needed for their examination, so eager is he to gather up the remainder of those priceless scripts which still lie buried in the sands of Northern Africa. The University of Pennsylvania likewise, as the result of a series of expeditions to the Far East, owns to-day a great unexplored Babylonian Library. These books in clay number many thousands, and it will occupy the life-time of probably a dozen experts to assort and decipher them. I select only these two instances out of many. One may well sympathize with the scholars who have to attack this huge mass of writings of all sorts,—drafted upon papyrus, parchment,

---

[1] Cp. Grenfell and Hunt's *Sayings of our Lord*. London, 1897. Also *The Oxyrhynchus Papyri*. London, 1898- . [*In progress.*]

wood and stone.   And the pile, huge as it is already, is constantly growing in bulk.   Far from having fairly accomplished his task, the material which still awaits the historian of religion is multiplying much more rapidly than it is being disposed of.   Instead, therefore, of wishing to engage in supererogatory inquiries, such workers are looking about them for the assistance necessary to lighten their quite overwhelming labours.   With the aid of the limited staff at present in the field, it is quite certain that their undertaking will never be completed : for the goal lies much further distant to-day than it did five years ago !

Accordingly, it is the proposal and the ambition of students of Comparative Religion to help to remove this difficulty.   That they do not personally collect the facts of religion does not prevent their making a legitimate and competent use of them.   They offer their services at the present juncture, animated by no wish to supplant the History of Religions, but moved by a desire to relieve it of part of its burden.   It seems to them a mistake and an injustice that the historian of religion should be constantly perplexed, and sometimes overwhelmed, by his attempt to carry a quite impossible load.   But a second consideration, not less important, has prompted the present attitude of students of Comparative Religion.   It is this : the historian in this field, even were he able to keep abreast of the work belonging to his own proper domain, furnishes no guarantee that Comparative Religion shall receive at his hands that exactitude of treatment which it requires and demands.   That the task will be performed hurriedly and inadequately needs no demonstration : in the circumstances, no other result is possible.   But will the investigation be conducted aright, *even so far as it goes?*   In the majority of cases, a negative answer is inevitable.   The valid comparison of the Faiths of mankind— not made by concentrating attention upon their superficial features of likeness or unlikeness, but executed in a far deeper and more penetrative way—is a task which not every scholar is competent to perform.   Comparison, in so far as the historian is concerned, is a passing incident, a detail, a side issue.   With the student of Comparative Religion, on the other hand, it is his one and supreme business.   It happens to be, moreover, an undertaking of extreme difficulty and subtlety, calling for skilled and careful treatment.   The facts which the historian supplies require in due course to be interpreted, and they must be interpreted by one who thoroughly understands them.   Such a teacher will be able to say with confidence what these facts MEAN—not what they *probably* mean, but what they *unquestionably* mean, when one reads unerringly their actual and authentic significance. It is quite unnecessary to labour the point that, if a scholar aspires to be accounted an authority in any department of knowledge, he must be willing to devote the major part of his time to the cultivation of *one subject only*. No real advance is possible in any science to-day without specialization. It is safe to go further and affirm that no accurate acquaintance with any branch of science is possible without at least some measure of specialization.

Hence, it is now beginning to be recognized that the equipment of a leader in Comparative Religion needs to be materially different from that demanded of an expert in the History of Religions. Both workers must possess indeed such endowments as comprehensive knowledge, catholicity of temper, exhaustless patience, and dauntless courage ; but the latter must, in addition, be conspicuously proficient in the use of the comparative method. It is felt, therefore, to-day—and to an ever increasing degree—that Comparative Religion must no longer be given over to the tender mercies of well-meaning but often very poorly qualified exponents. It must be delivered from the reproach which rested for a time so heavily upon the History of Religions itself, viz. the mischievous intermeddling of the dilettante scholar. The competency and ease with which the genuine expert in such work confronts and accomplishes his task is very different from the uncertain advances and withdrawals of those to whom such investigations are admittedly unfamiliar. A certain dexterity is essential ; and it can be acquired, like skill of other kinds, only by careful training under capable masters. It is for such interpreters that the science of Comparative Religion is now diligently searching. In the hands of scholars thus fitted for their work, it will soon become a highly specialized branch of human knowledge; it will easily demonstrate its right to occupy a distinct field of its own ; and (not least) it will indicate clearly the boundaries which separate it from those other sciences with which it is now frequently but short-sightedly confounded.

IV. *Some urgent desiderata, in view of the new claims advanced by Comparative Religion.*—The time has fully come when definitely constructive work ought to be undertaken in the interest of Comparative Religion. Many lines of advance are already open and inviting, but two at least must be emphasized in the present connexion.

1. An adequate and uniform definition of Comparative Religion.—

A more exact connotation must be attached, and without further postponement, to the name of this new science. Its official designation is at present being used in the most vague and confusing way. Not only does the inexact student employ the title in a characteristically careless manner, but—in the absence of a deliberate discrimination between contiguous spheres of inquiry—even reputable scholars are almost equally blameable in this particular. No general agreement has yet been reached touching the limits respectively of the History of Religions and Comparative Religion. Accordingly, some authorities of the first rank frequently use the two designations as if they were synonymous:[1] other authorities of equal standing set the two disciplines apart, but fail to assign to each of them precisely the same constituents. A brief definition of Comparative Religion, accepted and adhered to by all responsible teachers, would render immense service towards differentiating these two departments of research, each of which would then be restricted to an express and distinctive task.

The widely current employment of the title 'The Comparative History of Religions' shows that the domain of the History of Religions has already been overstepped. A new study has arisen

---

[1] Cp. *The New Schaff-Herzog Encyclopedia*, vol. i, p. 236. New York, 1908- .
[*In progress.*] Yet, in a subsequent volume of the same work, viz. in the advance sheets of the article on 'Comparative Religion', the latter designation is employed as if it were synonymous with 'The Science of Religion'. Professor Sanday holds that the History of Religions and Comparative Religion are 'substantially the same thing' (*Christianity and other Religions,*' p. 5. London, 1908). On the Continent, a similar confusion prevails. Every student knows the variety of meanings conveyed by such phrases as 'L'histoire comparée des religions,' 'La science des religions comparées,' 'Religione comparata,' 'Storia comparata delle religioni,' 'Vergleichende Religionsgeschichte,' 'Religionsvergleiche,' 'Religions-vergleichung,' &c. The interpretation of these titles must always be governed by a knowledge of the worker who chances to employ them ! Professor Söderblom would make 'Comparative Religion' synonymous with 'The Philosophy of Religion' (*Studiet Av Religionen*, p. 86. Stockholm, 1908). Count Goblet d'Alviella recommends the introduction of the terms Hierography and Hierology, the former being restricted to the descriptive history, and the latter to the comparative history, of the religions of mankind.
I am not sure that the distinction now being enforced is sufficiently emphasized in the Trust Deed of the new Wilde Lectureship, which has just been founded in the historic University of this city. It will always be a happily commemorative circumstance that, in the year of the meeting of this great Congress in Oxford, an instructor entered upon his duties as a teacher of 'Natural and Comparative Religion'. But the Deed accompanying this endowment reads : 'Comparative Religion shall be taken to mean the modes of causation, rites, observances and other concepts involved in the higher historical religions, as distinguished from the naturalistic ideas and fetishisms of the lower races of mankind.' Surely this definition is wide enough to include almost *every* important subdivision of the Science of Religion !

for which it is necessary to invent and adopt a new name. That science which has to do exclusively with the skilled application of the comparative method to the verified facts of religion is surely old enough already, and definite enough in its purpose, to be granted a sphere of its own. Even should the recognition of this just claim be somewhat further postponed, the present fluidity of meaning commonly associated with the name 'Comparative Religion' is in the highest degree unsatisfactory. This babel of tongues ought to cease. On the other hand, the study of the History of Religions, taken by itself, is confessedly incomplete. The data it accumulates must be authoritatively weighed and compared. In a word : the factor of comparison, hitherto employed in a somewhat promiscuous way, must in future be committed to the hands of competent and trusted experts.

2. *The systematic training of men who aspire to leadership in this field.*—The science of Comparative Religion, just because it *is* a science, means a good deal more than the placing of the Faiths of mankind side by side, and then (after one has compared and contrasted them) the framing of a formal estimate of their respective claims and values. Such an estimate, unless it be exact and exhaustive, is utterly worthless. It should be attempted only by those who are manifestly qualified to make it : for all scientific criticism demands something from those who venture to employ it, as well as from those who are asked to accept and respect it.

Such endowments as quickness of insight, accuracy of perception, and keenness in one's powers of discrimination are qualities which even the most skilful training cannot hope to impart. In the absence of gifts of this order, any student who offers himself as a candidate for this field is plainly barred. Nevertheless such talents, if possessed, can be immensely developed under judicious supervision and guidance. Moreover, confident employment of the comparative method—however natural and congenial such work may chance to be—can be secured only through experience. Experimental attempts at the comparison of religions must be conducted and repeated until they have ceased to be experiments. Only by the way of successive mistakes and failures can one hope to reach that pre-eminence from which mistakes and failures have successfully been eliminated. Individual aptitudes, whether constitutional or acquired, will then be utilized to their fullest capacity. Moreover, all the intellectual powers of the student, now rendered eager and acute, will be brought under effective control. Nay, yet further : these powers will be

found to be continually being supplemented by other mental
supports, and in such a manner as to augment immeasurably their
energy and worth.

The necessity of making provision for the express training of men
who desire to devote themselves to the promotion of Comparative
Religion brings under view a timely and extremely important subject.
It demands our serious attention.   I propose to devote to it,
accordingly, the remainder of this Paper.

Of the various expedients adopted thus far, only three need be
mentioned here.

(1) Special Professorships.—Some have thought that the establishment of one or more Professorships in a few representative universities
and theological seminaries ought sufficiently to meet the requirements
of the case.   This course has already, to a certain extent, been carried
into effect.   It has been followed, and with excellent results, in
Holland, France, England, and the United States.   The objection
however is well grounded that, in almost every instance, these new
Chairs have been assigned to the History of Religions, and Comparative Religion in consequence has been practically overlooked.
Honourable exceptions, happily, may be cited.   A Professorship in
Comparative Religion was founded in the University of Manchester
in 1904 : it will always enjoy the distinction of being the first—as it
remains to this hour the only—Chair of its kind in the British Isles.
A notable beginning has also been made in Oxford.   In addition to
the provision for this subject which had already been effected by the
University in this city—candidates in its Honour School of Theology
being permitted to select Comparative Religion as one of their
'optional' subjects—a new Lectureship in 'Natural and Comparative
Religion' has just been founded through the beneficence of a generous
benefactor.[1]

(2) Separate University Departments.—Another expedient adopted
with the view of providing competent workers in this field has taken
shape in the creation, in several foremost universities, of a separate
'Department'.   Within this Department, a group of professors
judiciously subdivide amongst themselves the leading branches of
inquiry proper to the critical study of religion.   In the United
States, this procedure has been initiated in quite a number of
instances.   Notable examples are Columbia University, Harvard

---

[1] Cp. p. 14.   It is a noteworthy fact that both Hon. Secretaries of this Congress
are Lecturers on Comparative Religion, the one (Principal Carpenter) a veritable
pioneer, seeing that he began this work more than thirty years ago, while the
other (Dr. Farnell) is to deliver his Inaugural in the early part of 1909.

University, Boston University, and the University of Chicago. It will be observed that this new move—suggested no doubt by the splendid work being accomplished on behalf of the History of Religions by the *École des Hautes Études* in Paris—is largely an American experiment. It presupposes a strong university staff, and is attended with considerable expenditure. It is only under exceptionally favourable conditions that this scheme is likely to be imitated.

(3) A Centrally-situated Training Institution.—I come now to speak of an expedient much more promising than the establishment of either local Professorships, or local Lectureships, or even the creation of separate University Departments. Instead of founding a few (more or less isolated) Chairs in a number of selected universities, why should not an effort be made to establish—in the chief national capitals—a central and well-endowed Institution, in which the work of scientific research in religion could be prosecuted in a broad and thoroughly scholarly manner? A corps of specialists— say ten or fifteen, devoting themselves (with genuine ardour and without dogmatic restraint) to the solution of all questions affecting in any way the development of the world's religions—could then give their whole time and thought to the advancement of this single line of inquiry. In such an Institution, Comparative Religion would not fail to receive a duly proportionate measure of attention. Moreover, all work of this character, at present prosecuted in a necessarily intermittent and casual sort of way, would quickly become systematized, consolidated, and rendered more than doubly productive.

Such a central School of Religion would duplicate no college now in existence. On the contrary, it would occupy towards existing Professorships, Lectureships, and Departments the relation which Comparative Religion properly holds to the History of Religions: it would carry contemporary investigations a step further forward. Nay—much more than 'a step'—it would carry such investigations a long stride forward! With a fullness of equipment for its special work which no purely local Institution could ever hope to rival, with a reference library and museum as complete as money could make them, it would be indeed a College of Specialists; and it would discharge a further important function through its training of additional specialists. Attended by a small number of picked graduate students—not necessarily or mainly theological students, but men whose alertness and openness of mind had singled them out for this distinction—the School would devote its whole strength to the furtherance of unfettered research.

If but one such Institution could be established and thoroughly equipped, it would not long stand alone. A sort of Clearing House for all the universities, fuller and more fruitful inquiry could be undertaken, and at considerably less outlay, than if twice its staff of professors were distributed over a number of selected centres. Why should any one country—America, for example—make itself responsible for twenty or thirty instructors in the History of Religions, most of whom (secluded, and often discouraged in their loneliness) would be engaged merely in duplicating aud reduplicating the work which others were doing? A central Laboratory, on the other hand, would courageously attack all especially difficult problems; it would authoritatively interpret multifarious facts belonging to the entire range of the field; it would be in effect a National Bureau of Religious Information; and it would publish an official Journal, besides other occasional books and periodicals of its own. All recent intelligence concerning the progress of the Science of Religion—in all its branches, and in all lands—would be promptly registered, and as promptly made known; and in this way the greatest present drawback affecting students in this field, viz. the lack of easy co-operation, would rapidly disappear. In particular, the interrelated 'Departments' of the Science of Religion would quickly become differentiated, their respective limits being confidently and sharply defined.

But the cost! Is not the scheme, however admirable, hopelessly Utopian?

By no means. The item of cost has never permanently blocked the advance of any really essential project. Over and over again have 'impossible' bridges been built and 'impossible' tunnels excavated, when it became manifest that such public highways were likely to prove profitable investments. Such undertakings, to be sure, involve great outlay: but, in view of the results to be achieved by and by, who grudges what they cost? And special Schools for the study of religion have become a modern necessity. It is not enough that facilities for the training of students in Comparative Religion already exist in various quarters: these forces must be made visible. They must be effectively combined. They must be skilfully marshalled. Nay, more: they must be magnified as well as multiplied. They must be made so prominent that many who to-day are *not* thinking of making Comparative Religion their life-work will be attracted, and ultimately enlisted in its service.

A study which is rapidly effecting a complete revolution in the

general estimate of the Ethnic religions, and of their relationship
not less to Christianity than to one another, may well engage the
interest and demand the assistance of all studious and large-hearted
men.   The publication of Dr. Hastings's latest achievement in the way
of a thoroughly modern Encyclopaedia [1] is a proof that the advent
of a new age is about to be marked by a fuller recognition of our
growing responsibilities.   This superb undertaking, the product
of the combined labours of experts of all nationalities, stands alone
to-day in point of accuracy, fullness, and up-to-dateness in every
particular.   There is nothing that even approaches it, in these
respects, in any modern language.   In Germany, one of the volumes
of a massive work, bearing the title *Die Kultur der Gegenwart*, has
been devoted exclusively to 'The Non-Christian Religions': [2] and
a still later but more compact Encyclopaedia, embracing both the
Christian and non-Christian faiths, is now in course of rapid
preparation. [3]   Other instances might be cited; indeed, there is
scarcely a theological dictionary of any grade published to-day that
does not profess to cover the field of Comparative Religion.   Even
so recently as five years ago, none of the standard cyclopaedias—
though running from ten to thirty volumes—found space for an
article on this theme: now even such works as are comprised
within a single volume are deemed incomplete without it !   But
in all these cases, while the element of comparison is by no means
ignored, [4] the treatment is mainly historical.   The writers are his-
torians, and they are probably wise in restricting themselves rigidly
to the lines of their own special investigations.   Something more is
demanded, however, and will yet be secured.   The project of founding
various Schools of Religion, in which the problems in question can
be dealt with systematically and fully, is not a dream merely, but
a dream that will one day become a visible and substantial reality.
When the occasion arrives, neither arguments nor advocates nor
financial backing will be wanting.   In the meantime, it is well to
bear in mind that good causes are won for the most part, not merely
because they deserve to win, but because of the earnestness, energy,
and patience of those who believe in them, and who are resolved to
secure and ensure their triumph.

[1] *Encyclopaedia of Religion and Ethics.*   10 vols.   Edinburgh, 1908- .   [*In
progress.*]

[2] *Die Orientalischen Religionen.*   Leipsic, 1906.

[3] *Die Religion in Geschichte und Gegenwart.*   4 or 5 vols.   Tubingen, 1908- .
[*In progress.*]

[4] In one notable publication of the current year, the fair promise of the Preface
is certainly not fulfilled in the pages that follow !

V. *Conclusion.*—At this point I must stop. No attempt has been made to give a complete view of the method and scope of Comparative Religion, or to present anything more than some memoranda bearing upon its distinctive purpose and policy. The topic of my Paper has restricted our survey to a study of the relationship which subsists between Comparative Religion and the History of Religions. Far from being able to agree with Professor Sanday in holding that these two branches of inquiry are 'substantially the same thing',[1] it seems to me that the procedure and range of Comparative Religion are essentially different from those of that earlier discipline from which it has sprung. The relation of Comparative Religion to the History of Religions may be said, broadly speaking, to correspond to the relation of the New Testament to the Old. Both of these venerable writings belong to the same body of documents, and therefore they are rightly bound up together in a single volume. Yet more striking than their essential interdependence is the evidence of their essential difference. The New Testament presupposes the Old, but at the same time it marks an immense advance beyond it. The continuity of the two Scriptures is unmistakable; but, to change the figure, the root of the growth they embody stands removed by a very considerable interval from its blossom and flower. The fruit of this sowing remains more distant still: it will no doubt be reaped some day in a mature and comprehensive Philosophy of Religion. In the meantime, the ordinary processes of development must be allowed to discharge their functions. The method of the historian must, first of all, fulfil *its* task. The scope of the historian's responsibility is limited by his method. But—lying outside of the historian's domain, and employing a method fitted to meet an entirely different demand—there stretches that field in which Comparative Religion is at work, and in which it is winning its reward. The facts, previously collected and verified, are there critically compared, and their various relationships are indicated and established. To have attained skill and confident progress in such an undertaking is to have passed beyond the frontier of the History of Religions. Consciously or unconsciously, one has already entered the territory of another science.

---

[1] Cp. footnote, p. 14.

CPSIA information can be obtained
at www.ICGtesting.com
Printed in the USA
BVHW071716280119
538842BV00035B/4417/P